MW01109345

"To face a life-thre
victorious takes God's
Butler has been there. She kn
a battle with cancer. This book is straight to the point
of what it will take to succeed. The content is strong
meat for the caregiver and the one receiving health
and wholeness. This book can mean the difference
between death and life. The key to any knowledge is
the application of it. 'Faith is the victory that overcomes
the world,' 1 John 5:4. This book will feed faith and
starve doubts."

—Billy Joe Daugherty, Pastor
Victory Christian Center
Tulsa, Oklahoma

"God's Word is the power needed to heal any
sickness of body, mind, or spirit. I believe that this book
provides the pure, undiluted Word of God in a manner
that is easy to apply in any circumstance, even to such
seemingly impossible situations as cancer. Use God's
Word and watch its miracle working power in action.
'For the word of God is living and active. Sharper than
any double-edged sword, it penetrates even to dividing
soul and spirit, joints and marrow; it judges the thoughts
and attitudes of the heart' Hebrews 4:12, NIV."

—Jerry Toops, PhD, LCSW
Director of Healing Ministries
First United Methodist Church
Tulsa, Oklahoma

"No other word can strike fear in a person or family member like the word "cancer." Judy Butler and her family fought and conquered their battle against cancer using the godly principles presented in this book. God is faithful to His Word and His Word works! As a professional pain management nurse, I cannot recommend this book ENOUGH! This book is timeless and is a MUST for any patient or caregiver faced with a diagnosis of cancer or life-threatening illness. Judy was near death's door when I met her at Cancer Treatment Center, and now she is cancer free!"

—Susan Brown, RN, BSN
Professional Pain Management Nurse
Cancer Treatment Centers of America
Tulsa, Oklahoma

"Inoperable, Incurable, Terminal ..."

HEALED!

Strength for Caregivers, Cancer Fighters, and Other Serious Illness Fighters

A Crash Course in What To Do Spiritually and Practically

ANGELA PETERSON

INCLUDES THE PERSONAL TESTIMONY
OF RON & JUDY BUTLER

—Large Print Edition—

Healed!
Strength for Caregivers, Cancer Fighters, and
Other Serious Illness Fighters
ISBN: 0-88144-303-4
Copyright © January 2009 by Angela Peterson

Supported by Butler Ministry Foundation

Thorncrown Publishing
A Division of Yorkshire Publishing Group
7707 East 111th, Suite 104
Tulsa, Oklahoma 74133
www.yorkshirepublishing.com

CONTENTS

INTRODUCTION

CANCER THROWS THE FIRST PUNCH

When you are first told your loved one has cancer, floods of emotions rush over your mind and heart in waves. Denial, horror, shock, numbness, depression, and heaviness like the weight of the world rolls over you again and again each minute. This is the beginning of your fight of faith. It sometimes is a short battle; but it can be a long, draining war. You will need several things to win this war and stay strong during this battle—realism, determination, hope, faith, rest, courage, support from others, Scriptures to stand on, and quiet time with God to rest in.

In October 1999, a team of medical specialists diagnosed my mother, Judy Butler, with "stage 4 colon cancer," the very last stage of one of the deadliest forms of cancer. Doctors said the first priority was emergency surgery to try to stop the massive hemorrhaging. If this was not successful, she had only two–three days to live. Even if she survived the surgery, the cancer itself could never be operated on because it was too large and had entwined itself around some major organs of her body. The doctor's only hope, medically, was to aggressively treat her with chemotherapy and radiation in hopes that would slow down the cancerous growth enough to give Judy more time—maybe two months—to live. The best of medical science could only prolong her death sentence. But God had a different plan for her! She was declared medically cancer free on April 17, 2000! Thank you, Lord! It is now 2004 and she continues to be monitored by physicians regularly and is still cancer free! Mom is extremely close to her only grandchild, Ashley, who was born after her battle with cancer.

ARE YOU TRAINED?

The Bible says, "My people are destroyed for *lack of knowledge*" (Hosea 4:6a). In the military, all soldiers are trained for battle. *Those who do not heed what their superior trains them to do* are more vulnerable to death and capture in war. But those who *are well trained* can achieve much for their country in battle, and if they die, they die as true heroes for the cause—honored champions crowned for obedience.

The same is true in a spiritual battle. "A final word: *Be strong* in the Lord and in his mighty power. *Put on all of God's armor* so that you will be able to stand firm against all strategies of the Devil. *For we are not fighting against flesh and blood enemies, but against evil rulers and authorities of the unseen world, against mighty powers in this dark world, and against evil spirits in the heavenly places*" (Ephesians 6:10–12 NLT).

Do you know how to fight for your God-given spiritual rights as listed in the Bible? This book is a crash course on what the real battle against sickness is and how to fight this battle and win. It worked for my family. It can work for yours.

CHAPTER 1

PREPARING FOR THIS SPIRITUAL AND PHYSICAL BATTLE

He sent his word, and healed them.

PSALMS 107:20A

TESTIMONY OF RON AND JUDY BUTLER

Ron and I married in 1964, and we have gone to church all of our lives. One day, not long after our wedding, we discussed what we had learned in church all those years. Ron remembered John 3:16, "For God so loved the world, that he gave his only begotten Son, that whosoever believeth in him should not perish, but have everlasting life." But I could not remember one Scripture!

Ron said, "Honey, you went to church for more than twenty years. Didn't you learn anything?"

"Well, I certainly *did!*" I exclaimed. "I remember a story about a man named Jonah, and he *swallowed a whale!*" I only remembered one story—and I got that one backwards.

Ron and I started talking about all the prayers we prayed throughout our lives, and neither one of us could remember a prayer we had prayed that had worked. Ron said if we had gone out to play football and not known any of the rules or regulations, we would have been pretty pathetic football players. Our prayer life had been pretty pathetic. He said, "We are going to learn to pray."

We bought a big concordance and made a large notebook of every Scripture in the Bible concerning prayer. We studied that like a textbook and we learned how to pray. We studied John 15:7, "If ye abide in me, and *my words* abide in you, ye shall ask what you will, and it shall be done unto you."

We realized we had no "words" in us—we had missed it. It was time for us to make a serious change. We started programming the Scriptures into our minds and hearts. We learned to pray to the Father in the name of "Jesus." Jesus says in John 16:23–24 (NIV), "In that day you will no longer ask me anything. I tell you the truth, my Father will give you whatever you ask in my name. Until now you have not asked for anything in my name. Ask and you will receive, and your joy will be complete."

We learned to pray and believe we received the answer *when we prayed*—not when it *came*. Mark 11:24b (NKJV) says, "Whatever things you ask for when you pray, believe that you receive *them*, and you will have *them*."

We learned Scripture after Scripture on prayer. Then we made a notebook on healing, and we learned Scriptures that said Jesus died on a cross for our salvation and also for all our sickness and disease including Isaiah 53:5, Matthew 8:16–17, and 1 Peter 2:24.

After being extremely healthy all my life in January, 1999, I was suddenly ill—and very ill. I saw doctors, but was mis-diagnosed until July, 1999. Ron put me in the hospital. They said, "She's got to have surgery. She probably won't live through surgery, but she's not going to live without it."

So they put me in surgery the next day, sewed me back up, and then told Ron and my family that I had "inoperable, incurable, terminal cancer in the fourth stage."

Ron said, "How many stages are there?"

They said, "Four."

He said, "What does that mean?"

"It means she doesn't have any time left."

One of my specialists said, "I've been working with a patient who had a condition identical to yours and in the same stage, except she is ten years younger than you. She died two weeks ago."

When the doctor said, "The cancer is so large and so involved in your organs that we cannot touch it," the Scripture came up so loud inside of me that says, "He sent *his word,* and healed them, and delivered *them* from their destructions" (Psalms 107:20). Then the Scripture came to me that says, "My son, attend unto *my words;* incline thine ear unto my sayings. Let them not depart from thine eyes; keep them in the midst of thine heart. For they are life unto those that find them, *and health to all their flesh*" (Proverbs 4:20–22).

For the next couple of months I got worse and worse. I lost fifty pounds and became just skin and bones. I was admitted to the Cancer Treatment Centers of America hospital in Tulsa, Oklahoma. It was not long until I became paralyzed from the waist down. I could not walk or even stand because the cancer had spread to my spine and my lymph nodes. At one time, they were afraid it was spreading to my brain.

I am a living example of the Word healing me. Five specialists who treated me said that I was a miracle—I could not have lived. But the Words of God brought life to my body and health to all of my flesh. God is God and His Word works. I was declared totally cancer-free on April 17, 2000. I continued to recover until October, 2001. During that time the doctors discontinued 23 medications and removed my internal epidural pain pump.

I encourage you to put the Word of God into your life on a daily basis. Read it; study it; meditate on it. The Word and Jesus are the same—John 1:14 says, "And the Word was made flesh, and dwelt among us, (and we beheld his glory, the glory as of the only begotten of the Father,) full of grace and truth."

Living in the Word of God is the most exciting and most powerful life you will ever have.

Ron

First of all, I want to thank everyone for the cards, letters, and e-mails. Some of them came at the most sensitive and most opportune times. You will never know how much those words of encouragement really lift people up who are struggling just to live each day.

During your lifetime, you may face situations you could never have imagined. This is my prayer of thanksgiving for Judy's healing, and I would like you to join me. As I say this prayer, repeat these words to yourself and make it your prayer too.

"Father, God, thank You for Your Son, Jesus, who died for my sins and was raised from the dead by Your mighty power. Jesus, You are my Savior, my Healer, and my Lord. Father, forgive me of my sins and all my past mistakes. And thank You for the free gift of eternal life. In Jesus' name, amen." God bless you and your family.

CHAPTER 2

HOW TO USE YOUR SPIRITUAL ARMOR

Ephesians 6:13–18 NLT lists the pieces of spiritual armor we have in the Lord.

> Therefore, put on every piece of God's armor so you will be able to resist the enemy in the time of evil. Then after the battle you will still be standing firm. Stand your ground, putting on the sturdy belt of truth and the body armor of God's righteousness. (6:13–14 NLT)

The word "righteousness" means "right-standing with God." It is God's free gift to you when you accept Jesus Christ as your Lord. It comes from *true* repentance of sins and the grace of God that Jesus brings to your life.

For shoes, put on the peace that comes from the Good News so that you will be fully prepared (6:15). The "Good News" is the knowledge of Jesus Christ and His salvation for every person.

In addition to all of these, hold up the shield of faith to stop the fiery arrows of the devil. *Put on salvation as your helmet, and take the sword of the Spirit, which is the word of God. Pray in the Spirit at all times and on every occasion. Stay alert and be persistent in your prayers for all believers everywhere.* (6:16–18 NLT)

Notice the only offensive weapon we have is the sword of the Spirit—the Word of God. By saying the Scriptures about healing over your life, you are offensively attacking sickness and disease. The rest of the armor is defensive: the belt of truth, the breastplate of righteousness, the shoes of peace, the shield of faith, the helmet of salvation. Those weapons will help you to stand strong in faith even when circumstances look impossible.

The Bible says in 2 Chronicles 20:15b, "Thus saith the Lord … the battle is not yours, but God's."

It is hard to keep that in mind except by reading it and saying it daily.

The commandment given most frequently by Jesus is *"Fear not."* Remember that. Fear is our enemy—it breaks your concentration on the positive, tears your lifeline of hope for recovery, and breaks your emotional stamina.

When you are in this fight of faith, you don't have the luxury of fear. If you trust what God said in His Word and do what He said to do, you have a great chance for a miracle. I can't explain why some are healed and some are not when it seems they are doing everything according to the Bible. But I know this: if you fear and refuse to believe or act upon God's Word, you have a very small chance of receiving a miracle.

The Bible is our instruction book on how to live by God's laws. Yes, there are spiritual laws just as there are laws of nature. A seed planted in the ground will produce after its own kind. Gravity will pull objects towards the earth. And when you *study God's Word day and night* and obey what is written in it, you will prosper and have success (Joshua 1:8).

Mark 11:23 tells us *to say to the mountain* (of sickness), "Be removed and cast into the sea."

Believe when you pray that you will have whatever you say (Mark 11:24).

Confess your sins and ask forgiveness with true repentance (1 John 1:9).

Forgive others so you may be forgiven and your prayers will be answered (Mark 11:26).

Lay hands on the sick and they will recover (Mark 16:18).

Anoint them with oil in the name of the Lord. Call for the elders of the church. Pray one for another (James 5:14–15).

Give and it shall be given unto you (Luke 6:38), so pray for other patients. You will see many of them in various waiting rooms as you go to different tests and examinations. Smile at these patients; greet them and tell them you will pray for them—then do it. *If you make the Kingdom of God your primary concern,* God will take care of your daily needs—food, drink, and clothing (Matthew 6:19–33).

YOUR DEFENSIVE ARMOR

Ephesians 6:13 tells us to *"put on every piece of God's armor* so you will be able to resist the enemy in the time of evil. Then after the battle you will still be standing firm."* There are times in a battle when you are not making forward strides but are standing firm to hold your ground and resist retreating. It is the same in a spiritual battle.

The belt of truth means to acknowledge reality—both in the spiritual and the natural realm. The truth is that we have been healed by Jesus' wounds. He took our place on the cross (1 Peter 2:24 and Isaiah 53:5).

The truth is that the thief's (or Satan's) purpose is to steal, kill, and destroy. Jesus' purpose is to give life in all its fullness (John 10:10). The truth is that the devil has attacked your loved one with sickness. The truth is that God has given mankind science, technology, and wisdom along with faith, hope, and prayer. Use what He has given us! Using one gift does not negate the abilities of the other gift.

The truth is that all doctors do not treat cancer in the same manner, nor do they all treat cancer patients and their loved ones in the same manner.

Ask cancer survivors about their doctors—get good referrals. The same is true for any life-threatening disease.

The truth is, cancer is not an enemy to be toyed with; it fights hard and fast. Don't waste time living in denial, because with a life-threatening illness, *every day counts.*

The truth is, if we had found Cancer Treatment Centers of America (CTCA) when Mom was first diagnosed, we would have been way ahead of the game and saved her much pain and fatigue. Don't procrastinate. Be offensive against cancer. Be truthful in the natural and spiritual, although at times it seems hard to make those two coexist. Believe for a miracle, but be prudent about the treatments available.

The truth is, along with prayer and medical treatments, there are other treatments of merit including nutritional therapy, positive visualization, peaceful atmosphere, confessions (the words you speak at any time), and Scriptures—which are "God's medicine."

We found CTCA in Tulsa, Oklahoma, and we were amazed at the difference in attitude and treatment they presented. I would recommend them to anyone I know who is fighting cancer.

Also, realize if you choose to receive no medical treatment but want pain management, there are doctors who will gladly provide that, including Dr. Sorenson at CTCA in Tulsa. He will forever be my favorite doctor in the world. He and his nurses, Susan and Mac, were truly sent by God to us. No one understands the horror of watching a loved one suffer and being helpless to ease his or her pain like the caregivers.

Find a good pain management doctor as soon as possible, even if you do not currently need his or her services. Again, you don't know if this will be a quick win for your loved one or a long battle. You need to be diligent to be prepared for every situation. Find a good specialist doctor, even if you and/or your loved one are still praying as to what treatments to receive.

God's medicine is His Word, which we spoke confidently about Mom and to Mom in our conversations, and we prayed the Scriptures over Mom multiple times every day. Mom spoke these Scriptures loudly and boldly, literally all day long, every day for months. When Dad came home after work, he would do this with her. When I came over or her sisters or close friends came over, we would do this with her. When she became too weak to do so, one of us spoke them to her and over her aloud multiple times per day and she would say "Yes" or "I agree" when she was physically able.

The Scriptures we used are listed in the back of this book. You may feel silly doing it, but which is more important? Not feeling silly or embarrassed or fighting for your loved one's life by doing what God said in His Word (the Bible) to do? This is war—a spiritual battle. Don't let your mind talk you out of fighting; don't be a defector. Be a warrior.

YOUR HELMET OF SALVATION

John 3:16–17 says, "For God so loved the world that he gave his one and only son, that whoever *believes in him* shall not perish but have eternal life. For God did not send his Son into the world to condemn the world, but to save the world through him" (NIV).

"For everyone has sinned; we all fall short of God's glorious standard" (Romans 3:23 NLT). But

Jesus, being made a sacrifice for us, brought us back into a relationship with God. Romans 10:8–10 explains how to become a Christian. If you have not given your life to Christ, please read this passage. At the end of chapter 1 of this book there is a prayer of salvation, and by sincerely praying those words, you can receive Jesus as your Lord right now. "But what does it say? *'The word is near you, in your mouth and in your heart'* (that is, the word of faith which we preach): that if you confess with your mouth the Lord Jesus and believe in your heart that God has raised Him from the dead, you will be saved. For with the heart one believes unto righteousness, and with the mouth confession is made unto salvation" (NKJV).

Sin separates us from God. Jesus paid the price with his perfect life as a pure sacrifice on the cross for us. When we accept Jesus into our life and heart, we are back in relationship with our creator, Father God.

YOUR BREASTPLATE OF RIGHTEOUSNESS

The word "righteousness" means to be right with God. None of us can be righteous without Jesus Christ. We all sin in various ways and must continually turn from these sins and sincerely ask God's forgiveness and ask for His help to refrain from repeating them. Righteousness comes from true repentance of sins—things we have done that are wrong or bad.

The Bible talks about the importance of forgiveness—both for us to forgive others and for us to judge ourselves and ask forgiveness for our sins on an ongoing basis. 1 John 1:8–10 reads, "If we claim we have no sin, we are only fooling ourselves and not living in truth. *But if we confess our sins to him,* he is faithful and just to forgive us our sins and to cleanse us from all wickedness. If we claim we have not sinned, we are calling God a liar and showing that his word has no place in our hearts" (NLT).

It is just as important to forgive yourself as it is to forgive others because unforgiveness of any kind hinders us from moving forward in our walk with God. You also need to realize that *unforgiveness itself is a sin!* Unforgiveness of yourself or others robs you of health and happiness both spiritually and physically.

The Bible says (Proverbs 17:22) a merry heart is good medicine, but a broken spirit saps a person's strength. A merry heart requires the joy of Lord. Mark 11:25–26 says *when you stand praying*, forgive so that your father in heaven may forgive you.

I think it is significant that righteousness is listed as the breastplate, which in our bodies covers our natural hearts. Righteousness saves our spiritual "heart," our spirit, our soul—who we really are inside that body!

YOUR FEET SHOD WITH THE PREPARATION OF THE GOSPEL OF PEACE

Are you wearing your spiritual shoes? Or are you barefoot trying to fight a war? Soldiers wouldn't be very prepared if they went to the battlefield without their shoes, would they? Shrapnel, thorns, thistles, snakes, spiders, and all kinds of things would soon cause pain to their feet and affect their performance.

Prepare for your battles throughout the day by studying the Scriptures about peace, God's faithfulness, healing, forgiveness, and faith. Studying the Word with casettes or CDs of strong preachers, books, and other materials will build and maintain your faith through this war and bring peace to your mind (Ephesians 6:15). A peaceful environment is very important for your loved one as well. You must protect him or her from too much exciting stimulation—whether it be positive or negative. Any kind of excitement can increase pain levels, even when on pain medication.

Put on your spiritual shoes and protect the feet you are standing upon so you may stand firm and go forward in this spiritual war against cancer or whatever disease you are fighting. You may not win every battle—Mom had to have an emergency colostomy; she actually got worse before she was totally healed. There were nights we thought we would lose her. *BUT YOU CAN WIN THIS WAR!* Mom is cancer free. She has been tested on a regular basis and has been medically declared cancer free since April 17, 2000. Praise God!

YOUR SHIELD OF FAITH

Ephesians 6:16 says that *in every battle you will need faith as your shield* to stop the fiery arrows aimed at you by Satan. The New King James Version states the shield of faith causes you to "quench all the fiery darts of the wicked one." Hebrews 11:1–2 says, "Now faith is being sure we will get what we hope for. It is being sure of what we cannot see. God was pleased with the men who had faith who lived long ago" (NLV).

What is faith? It is the confident assurance that what we hope for is going to happen. It is the evidence of things we cannot yet see. God gave his approval to people in days of old because of their faith. Faith protects your salvation, righteousness, health, and peace. Without faith, you cannot be saved or be righteous (in right standing with God after repenting of sin).

"For just as the body without the spirit is dead, so also faith without works is dead" (James 2:26 NASB). "Works" are God-inspired good deeds. All of the book of James, chapter 2, is very helpful. It is impossible to please God without *faith* (Hebrews 11:6).

In Mark 13:31 Jesus says, "Heaven and earth will disappear, but my words will never disappear" (NLT). God is not a man that He can lie (Numbers 23:19 NIV), so His Words ARE the truth and are more permanent than the circumstances (cancer or any sickness) you currently see.

Continually, boldly reading the Scriptures about healing will increase your faith. Refuse to listen to negative people who do not believe you or your fighter will be healed. Do not let negative words or doctor reports get into your heart. You cannot afford to do that, and neither can your fighter. When you feel your shield of faith start to drop, renew your strength to uphold it through studying the Word and saying Scriptures and positive words over yourself and/or your loved one.

I went through a couple of weeks when Mom got progressively worse in which I was mad at God. I felt He had abandoned us and that He was not honoring Mom's faith and stance for her life, nor that of us, the caregivers.

It was hard for me to pray during that time. I had to struggle to make myself confess the Scriptures over and over because it looked like nothing we were doing was working. But Dad said something that helped me come back and ask God to forgive me. He said something like, "If you lose your faith in God's will to heal her, or turn from Him completely, the consequences of not believing in God are living a life with no faith in—or help from—God, and going to hell when you die. Those consequences are much worse than believing in Him and trusting in His sovereignty if He lets her die—even though we did all we could tell we were supposed to do according to the Bible. When we are doing our best to do all that the Bible instructs us to do, we and Mom will be 'good and faithful servants' and will have rewards in heaven for doing the right things and being faithful, even if we lose her now." (See Matthew 25:23.) *The Bible tells us to pray fervently in faith.*

> Are any of you sick? *You should call for the elders of the church to come and pray over you, anointing you with oil in the name of the Lord. Such a prayer offered in faith* will heal the sick, and the Lord will make you well, and if you have committed sins, you will be forgiven. *Confess your sins to each other and pray for each other* so that you may be healed. The *earnest prayer of a righteous person* has great power and produces wonderful results. Elijah was a human as we are, and yet when he prayed earnestly that no rain would fall,

none fell for the next three and a half years! Then, when he prayed again, the sky sent down rain and the earth began to yield its crops. (James 5:14–18 NLT)

The Bible says to have faith, to speak the right words and confessions, and to not faint (see verses in chapter 5). As it says in Galatians 6:9, "*So don't get tired of doing what is good.* At just the right time we will reap a harvest of blessing *if we don't give up*" (NLT).

It is our responsibility to obey these command-ments in the Bible to the best of our ability. You can always come back to God and He will be faithful and just to forgive you and cleanse you from all unrighteousness (1 John 1:9). If you get mad at God like I did, PLEASE, I beg you, come back to Him for the sake of yourself and your loved ones. If you are the caregiver and you stop fighting, the chances of winning the war are much less. Don't give regret and grief a chance to harass you for the rest of your life.

If you are the fighter, stay strong. God is more than able to do the impossible. Trust Him no matter how you feel. Refuse to give up.

CHAPTER 3

TO WIN YOU MUST STOP WORRY AND FEAR

We are human. You will have moments of fearful and tearful emotions, but do not allow yourself to dwell on them for long. Force yourself to return to what God says about you and/or your loved one. Tell the fighter's body it must line up with the Word of God, which states that by Jesus' stripes you are healed (1 Peter 2:24).

Speak to the cancer or the sickness and tell it to leave, because you give it no place in your family. Ephesians 4:27 says, "Neither *give place to the devil.*" It wouldn't say that if we did not have the *ability* to give him a place to come into our lives. We "give him place" by committing sins—even white lies, half-truths, rudeness, lingering anger, or gossip.

To live in God's plan we must strive to think on good things. Philippians 4:8 says, "Fix your thoughts on what is true, and honorable, and right, and pure, and lovely, and admirable. Think about things that are excellent and worthy of praise" (NLT). We must also live our lives in His kind of love, as stated throughout Ephesians and 1 Corinthians 13.

The Bible says to submit yourself to God; resist the devil and he must flee (James 4:7). Be a doer of the Word and resist the devil. Tell the devil and cancer or sickness of any kind that you are resisting it and will not accept it.

Mom chose to take communion almost daily for a while because she felt God was telling her to do so. Communion is a sacrament whereby you repent of and confess your recent sins and ask God to forgive you and help you change so that you don't continue repeating those sins. (See 1 Corinthians 11:23–32.)

Please realize that the "spiritual world"—the constant battle between God (good) and Satan/devil (evil)—is more real than what we see in our "real" or natural world we live in. What the Bible says about you or your fighter (you are healed through Jesus' dying on the cross) is *more true* and more real than the sickness you see in you or your loved one.

When Jesus was tempted by Satan in the wilderness, He refuted Satan's attack by responding with this Scripture: "It is written, *'Man shall not live by bread alone, but by every word that proceeds from the mouth of God'*" (Matthew 4:4 NKJV). You cannot be moved by what you see, but from the Word of God in the Bible. Whether or not you choose to believe and do what God says in the Bible, the facts are still the same—God's way is still the only way, no matter what you and I choose to believe or do.

A minister whom I admire encouraged me that our outer self (appearance, clothes, wealth, public words and deeds, smiles) is our reputation with others, but our inner self (attitudes, thoughts, desires, will, private words and deeds) is our reputation with God—and it is the more important reputation. Joshua 1:9 says, "Be strong and be courageous! Do not be afraid or discouraged. For the Lord your God is with you wherever you go" (NLT).

BE A DOER OF THE WORD AND NOT A HEARER ONLY

James 1:22 says, "But don't just listen to God's Word. *You must do what it says. Otherwise, you are only fooling yourselves*" (NLT). I am a person who is task oriented. Maybe you are also the type of person who needs to be doing something to feel productive, but even if you are not, the following action steps will bring results.

State your loved one's case by saying the healing Scriptures located at the end of this book and any other Scriptures God impresses upon you, day and night, in the car, in the shower, when you wake up, and when you go to bed.

Organize a Prayer Priority Sheet that addresses the fighter's specific needs, and send it to everyone you believe will pray about those issues. Revise it often—weekly or daily as the needs change.

I have included Mom's Prayer Priority Sheet in the appendix at the back of this book as a sample for you. We mailed and faxed this sheet to every-one we knew who would pray for and believe in her healing.

We distanced ourselves from everyone who would not understand or be supportive of our faith stance for her healing, including people who said, "At least God has given you this time with her— enjoy the time you have left; I hope she makes it; etc." Dust those words off of you and move on as it says in Matthew 10:14: "If anyone will not welcome you or listen to your words, shake the dust off your feet when you leave that home or town" (NIV). *Do not let what they say affect you and your faith. Forgive them and move forward.*

YOUR LOVED ONE'S BELIEFS HAVE THE FINAL SAY

Keep in mind that if you are the caregiver and your loved one does not fight this fight with you, his or her chances for winning the battle are less. The caregiver does not have spiritual control over someone else's spiritual life. (The only time I can tell this is different is when the fighter is a child—the parents have spiritual authority over the child just as they have natural authority over him or her.) God gave each of us a choice, a free will, and we are all responsible for our own choices.

God is still God—He is sovereign and you must trust Him. We don't know why some recover and some do not. This is the hardest lesson for me, because I work in a "systems mentality"—if you do A and B, then you are guaranteed C. That may not always be true with God. There are so many factors involved in battling a terminal illness. However, it stands to reason that if we do all we know to do (A and B), we will have a much better chance at getting C than if we don't do A and B. So, do all you know to do through God's instruction book (the Bible), and then you can have confidence that you did your best and you will have no regrets or guilt.

One thing my husband and I did, as a sacrifice to God, to show Him our commitment—to "fight the good fight for what we believe" (1 Timothy 6:12)—for Mom's healing was to fast (abstain) from our favorite foods until she was cancer free. I gave up desserts and he gave up chips! This lasted almost six months.

I cannot say this is something required for everyone by any means, but God may impress upon you to do certain things during this war. You don't need to tell people you are doing something, but if you feel God is prompting you to do something, by all means—do it! Even if you are not sure it is God, if it does not go against the Bible or God's principles, I would do it just in case it *is* God! Better safe than sorry for me.

There are Scriptures about fasting, and it is a serious, spiritual time. I strongly suggest you read books by Billy Joe Daugherty on the subject before you decide to fast, because it is more in-depth spiritually than one might think. Fasting can be dangerous if done incorrectly.

Finally, we are responsible to be obedient to God and do what the Bible says to do—pray, forgive, confess, and love. We are only responsible to be obedient. If you are a caregiver and your loved one dies, you were still obedient and did your part—God will reward you and your loved one for "fighting the good fight of faith" (2 Timothy 4:7 NKJV) in heaven. God is sovereign and we cannot foresee the future as He does.

CHAPTER 4

PRACTICAL ASSISTANCE DURING THIS BATTLE

FOOD AND PROTEIN INTAKE IS IMPORTANT

Keep your health and help the fighter keep his or hers. Eat right, and take walks or do other exercise to refresh your body, mind, and emotions. Notice which good foods the fighter likes during the current stage of the battle, and be sure to have those foods on hand at all times.

Protein builds the immune system, and carbohydrates are good for energy. Protein shakes, peanut butter, cream of wheat, pasta, tomato soup, chicken noodle soup, and other nonspicy foods tasted okay to Mom during the worst part of the fight. You must remind the fighter that he or she is not eating for fun but eating to live. *Food is only medicine and must be eaten often whether the fighter is hungry or not.*

We would run to all sorts of restaurants and fast-food places to get something that sounded good to Mom, and we kept a variety of snacks in her room that she would nibble on. People tend to eat more when served food on large plates (so the portion of food looks smaller) and when others eat with them (humans are social eaters). Serve six to ten small meals per day to keep the fighter's weight and strength up. If the fighter is too nauseated or refuses to eat, ask your doctor about intravenous feeding until he or she is healthier.

Vitamins, herbs, and other remedies should be researched. Mom took selenium, vitamin C, vitamin E, potassium, soy protein, beta-carotene, a food enzyme to aid in digestion, and an antioxidant blend.

It may be helpful when going through chemotherapy and radiation to avoid metal bowls, pots, pans, and utensils when preparing food for your loved one since metal can change the flavor of foods to them during this time. Use plastic and glass.

We were told that cancer is a sugar-feeder so Mom should avoid eating refined sugar. However, if the only things she would eat contained sugar, we encouraged Mom to eat them anyway. We kept a list of foods that sounded good to her so we could remind her of them when her short-term memory was affected by the pain medication, and this made it much easier and faster for her to choose a food to eat. One needs to have some protein or fat (milk, butter) with any sugary food. To help your loved one eat more, use the optical illusion of placing all meals on huge plates. This makes the amount of food seem smaller. Have your loved one converse with someone or watch TV while eating—we all tend to eat more when we are preoccupied or entertained while doing so.

PILL-TAKING TIPS

Mom was never a good pill-taker because of her strong natural gag reflex. A nurse showed us how some pills and vitamins could be crushed into applesauce to help her get them in her system.

Some things can be taken through an IV or as a shot. Whenever possible, we had the medication given to Mom through a shot or IV, because if she took a pill and then threw up (which happened often), they could not give her another pill until the next scheduled time. They were unable to determine how much (if any) of the pill she ingested.

Usually, the pills were pain pills, and it was very important for her quality of life that she did not risk throwing up the painkiller and have to endure until the next scheduled pill. There are also places that make medicine in liquid forms for people with this problem—ask your doctor or nurse if you are interested. Selenium has so little taste that we poured the powder into her protein shakes, and that worked well for Mom.

BE PROACTIVE

Know your fighter's allergies and what drugs he or she is currently taking. I am still amazed that with a huge patient file sitting next to them, nurses and doctors would ask us what allergies Mom had and what medicines she was taking rather than looking in the chart. Do not assume that the next nurse, doctor, or anesthesiologist will be told these things. If you notice an emotional or physical change, let the nurse or doctor know because it may be due to a new medicine or anesthesia.

Don't assume anything. Be proactive. Even with great care like the kind Mom received, we still caught little things that slipped through the cracks. We are all humans—even medical staff. Be bold and ask questions and confirm certain things are being done. Ask for help from the nurses and doctors when needed. Your fighter is depending on you because often he or she cannot think clearly enough or doesn't have the strength to do things alone.

We also stayed with Mom in the room almost constantly. We had several friends and family members who did this with us, and we will cherish them forever for being there in our greatest time of need.

Call on family and friends you can trust to be positive and bold in what needs to be done, and ask them to take turns staying with your fighter. It is wise to have pen and notepad at all times so you or your help can write down all that the doctors and staff say. Keep a running list of foods and quantities of foods and liquids the fighter ate or drank and at what time he or she had them. Track the time, amount, and name of each medicine the fighter took in a notebook. Make sure you include vitamins and other supplements.

Even people who usually can accurately recall events from their memory may struggle with memory in this situation. I believe this is due to the stress and is a tactic of the enemy in the ongoing battle of good versus evil.

Write everything down and check things off the list as they are performed on your schedule. Have a list of allergies, a list of medicines and times to be administered, and Scriptures to read aloud ready for your helper so "fresh troops" can take the front line for a while and you can rest and recuperate. Train your helpers on what needs to be done so they feel confident they know what to do and what to ask the staff. You can't do it all and you cannot afford to become ill—take care of yourself.

Protect your fighter from the noise and over-excitement of too many or unexpected visitors. Germs from others are dangerous for your loved one too. We placed a note on the door that read, "Please, No Unexpected Visitors. Thank You for Understanding—The Family." Don't worry about what others think; be kind but be protective of the needs of your fighter. Be a leader.

Remember, this is much worse for your fighter than it is for you. This may be the most terrible thing you have ever gone through—it was for me. Even so, remember how much worse it is for your loved one. This is not a time for self-centeredness or self-pity.

If your loved one needs to talk about dying or living wills or "why is this happening to me" issues—as hard as it is for you—be there for your loved one and listen to what he or she is saying. Give your loved one permission to die if he or she chooses to, so your loved one doesn't die feeling he or she let you down. You do not want to live with the regret of letting your loved one die feeling that way. "No regrets" is how I try to approach hard decisions in my life. When you cannot decide how to respond to or handle a situation, consider which decision will leave you with the fewest regrets. The conscience is usually a good gauge of right and wrong, so listen to it.

You will have little time to do anything but read, study, confess, and build up your faith and your fighter's faith day and night. Cancer does not rest, and neither can you in your fight.

Dad bought a cassette player that turns to the other side when one side has finished playing, and we played positive tapes of ministers and songs of faith in Mom's room all night long, most nights. Praise and worship decreased pain. Worship and singing praises to the Lord with others chased pain away when nothing else would.

Remember to have a good pain management doctor and to call on him or her whenever needed. Home health assistance is also available. When Mom was home, CTCA helped arrange a nurse to come several times per week to dress the pain-pump incision and check on her condition. Know your options in this area.

The name of Jesus is above the name of cancer—"Jesus" is a higher name, a greater name, and a stronger name than "cancer." The Bible says in John 16:23–24, "The truth is, you can go directly to the Father and ask him, and he will grant your request because you use my name. You haven't done this before. Ask, using my name, and you will receive, and you will have abundant joy" (NLT). This was when Jesus was telling them how to pray to the Father using His name (as a proxy, if you will) as Jesus was preparing to leave the earth. Other Scriptures about the power of the name of Jesus are listed in the last chapter.

CHAPTER 5

SCRIPTURES TO BOOST YOUR HOPE, FAITH, AND STRENGTH

Please notice that *we are responsible* for the underlined sections; God is responsible for the rest when we obey and perform our part. Unless otherwise stated, all Scriptures in this chapter are from the New Living Translation of the Holy Bible.

BE SURE YOU AND YOUR LOVED ONE ARE SAVED

John 3:15–18

So that everyone who believes in him will have eternal life. For God loved the world so much that he gave his one and only Son, so that every-one who believes in him will not perish, but have eternal life. God sent his Son into the world not to judge the world, but to save the world through him. There is no judgment against anyone who believes in him. But anyone who does not believe in him has already been judged for not believing in God's one and only Son.

Isaiah 55:6

Seek the Lord while you can find him. Call on him now while he is near.

2 Peter 3:9

The Lord isn't really being slow about his promise, as some people think. No, he is being patient for your sake. He does not want anyone to be destroyed, but wants everyone to repent.

1 John 1:8–9

If we claim we have no sin, we are only fooling ourselves and not living in the truth. But if *we confess our sins to him,* he is faithful and just to forgive us our sins and to cleanse us from all wickedness.

John 5:24 (Jesus speaking)

"I tell you the truth, *those who listen to my message and believe in God who sent me* have eternal life. They will never be condemned for their sins, but they have already passed from death into life."

Romans 10:8–10

In fact it says, "The message is very close at hand; it is on your lips and in your heart." And that message is the very message about faith that we preach: If *you confess with your mouth that Jesus is Lord and believe in your heart that God raised him from the dead,* you will be saved. *For it is by believing in your heart* that you are made right with God, *and it is by* confessing with your mouth that you are saved.

Ephesians 2:8–9

God saved you by his grace when *you believed. And you can't take credit for this;* it is a gift from

God. Salvation is not a reward for the good things we have done, so none of us can boast about it.

The basic principles are: God loves you, sin separates people from God, and Jesus died for your sins. You can receive Jesus and experience God's love and forgiveness. This is how you are saved and how you go to heaven when you die, rather than experiencing eternal torment in hell for denying Jesus. In light of this truth, read Romans 10:8–10 again as well as 1 John 1:8–9.

PRAYER FOR SALVATION OR RENEWED COMMITMENT TO JESUS

To receive Jesus as your Lord, pray the following prayer out loud:

Heavenly Father, in Jesus' name, I repent of my sins. Please forgive me and help me turn from my sins and stop repeating the same wrongs. I ask Jesus to come inside my heart. Jesus, You are my Lord and Savior. I believe You are the Son of God and that You died for my sins and were raised from the dead. Fill me with Your Holy Spirit. Thank You, Father, for saving me.

2 Corinthians 5:17

This means that <u>anyone who belongs to Christ</u> has become a new person. The old life is gone; a new life has begun!

Now you must replace old bad habits with good habits that strengthen your heart/spirit with the knowledge/wisdom God gives us in the Bible.

WE MUST BE SELF-DISCIPLINED

Forcing Your Thoughts and Behavior to Line Up with God's Word

Proverbs 29:18

When people <u>do not accept divine guidance,</u> they run wild. *But <u>whoever obeys the law</u> is joyful.*

Romans 12:1–2

And so, dear brothers and sisters, I plead with you to *<u>give your bodies to God</u>* because of all he has done for you. *<u>Let them be a living and holy sacrifice</u>*—the kind he will find acceptable. This is truly the way to worship him. *<u>Don't copy the behavior and customs of this world,</u>* but let God *transform you into a new person by changing the way you think.* <u>Then you learn to know God's will</u> for you, which is good and pleasing and perfect.

Ephesians 4:22–24

<u>*Throw off your old sinful nature and your former way of life,*</u> which is corrupted by lust and deception. Instead, <u>let the Spirit renew your thoughts and attitudes.</u> *Put on your new nature,* created to be like God—truly righteous and holy.

Colossians 3:9–14

<u>*Don't lie to each other,*</u> for you have stripped off your old sinful nature and all its wicked deeds. <u>*Put on your new nature and be renewed*</u> as you <u>*learn*</u> to know your Creator and <u>become</u> like him. In this new life, it doesn't matter if you are a Jew or a Gentile, circumcised or uncircumcised, barbaric, uncivilized, slave, or free. *Christ is all that matters,* and he lives in all of us. Since God chose you to be the holy people he loves, <u>you must clothe yourselves with tenderhearted mercy, kindness, humility, gentleness, and patience. Make allowance for each other's faults, and forgive anyone who offends you.</u> Remember, the Lord forgave you, <u>so you must forgive others.</u> Above all, <u>clothe yourselves with love,</u> which binds us all together in perfect harmony.

Confession:

I will not limit God. He can do all things in   (name)   and through   (name)   because He is greater than our limitations. I will do what the Bible says to do in the fight against cancer/other illness for   (name) . Through God, we will be victorious. I refuse to think on the negative. We choose to believe what God's Word says about   (name) , and it says that by Jesus' stripes   (name)   is healed. So, I command his/her body to line up with the Word of God in Jesus' name.

GOD VALUES AND RESPECTS WORDS— BOTH HIS AND YOURS

Why Your Words, Statements, and Confessions are Important to God

There is something very important to God about *the words we choose to speak every day.* God made this planet *with words*—not deeds (Genesis 1). God's world works on words, faith, and love. Say these Scriptures out loud so you hear yourself saying them, and your faith will be greatly increased in a shorter amount of time. *Faith and words work in the same way for salvation as they do for healing. It is easy for most of us to accept the free gift of salvation and believe in it—try to receive the free gift of healing with the same simple faith.*

Proverbs 18:21

Words kill, words give life: they're either poison or fruit—<u>you choose.</u> (THE MESSAGE)

Matthew 12:37 (Jesus speaking)

Words are powerful; <u>take them seriously.</u> Words can be your salvation. Words can also be your damnation. (THE MESSAGE)

Isaiah 55:8–12a

"My thoughts are nothing like your thoughts," says the Lord. And my ways are far beyond anything you could imagine. For just as the heavens are higher than the earth, so are my ways higher than your ways and my thoughts higher than your thoughts. The rain and snow come down from the heavens and stay on the ground to water the earth. They cause the grain to grow, producing seed for the farmer and bread for the hungry. *It is the same with my word. I send it out, and it always produces fruit. It will accomplish all I want it to, and it will prosper everywhere I send it.* <u>*You will live in joy and peace.*</u>"

Proverbs 4:20–22

My child, <u>pay attention to what I say. Listen carefully to my words. Don't lose sight of them. Let them penetrate</u> deep into your heart, for they bring life to those who find them, and healing to their whole body.

Confession:

Father God, we are attending to Your Words. We are inclining our ears unto Your sayings and keeping them in front of our eyes. We keep them in our hearts. Your Words are life to __(name)__ and healing to all his/her flesh. We thank You for this promise and we are standing on this promise, as we fulfill our part.

Daniel 10:7–12

Only I, Daniel, saw this vision. The men with me saw nothing, but they were suddenly terrified and ran away to hide. So I was left there all alone to see this amazing vision. My strength left me, my face grew deathly pale, and I felt very weak. Then I heard the man speak, and when I heard the sound of his voice, I fainted and lay there with my face to the ground. Just then a hand touched me and lifted me, still trembling, to my hands and knees. And the man said to me, "Daniel, you are very precious to God, <u>so listen carefully to what I have to say to</u> you. <u>Stand up,</u> for I have been sent to you." When he said this to me, <u>I stood up,</u> still trembling. Then he said, "<u>Don't be afraid,</u> Daniel. Since the first day <u>you began to pray for</u>

understanding <u>and to humble yourself before</u> <u>your God,</u> your request has been heard in heaven. *I have come **in answer to your prayer.**"*

The New King James Version says, *"I have come **because of your words"*** (Daniel 10:12b).

Proverbs 4:23–24

<u>Guard your heart</u> above all else, for it *determines the course of your life.* <u>Avoid all perverse talk;</u> <u>stay away from corrupt speech.</u>

Joshua 21:45

Not a single one of all the good promises the Lord had given to the family of Israel was left unfulfilled; everything He had *spoken* came true.

Confession:

God, I believe that all Your promises are coming to pass in my life and in ___(name)___ 's life. Thank You for Your promises to us!

The following are Scriptures we spoke aloud to Mom and about Mom in the form of a confession of faith. Just insert the name of your fighter (or your own name) directly into the Scriptures and confessions, and boldly state these aloud over and over daily as though you are defending your rights at a legal trial.

Joel 3:10

Let the weak say, I am strong. (KJV)

Psalms 107:20

He _sent out his word and_ healed them, snatching them from the door of death.

Confession:

Thank you, God, for Your Word and for showing us how to use it as You planned. Thank You that as we speak Your Word over ___(name)___ and regarding ___(name)___, Your Word is healing ___(name)___ and delivering ___(name)___ from his/her destruction.

Psalms 103:1–5

Let all that I am praise the Lord; with my whole heart, I will praise his holy name. Let all that I am praise the Lord; may I never forget the good things he does for me. He forgives all my sins and heals all my diseases. He redeems me from death and crowns me with love and tender mercies. He fills my life with good things. My youth is renewed like the eagle's!

Confession:

*Say the following verses **with determination and passion.***

Psalms 107:1–2

(I) <u>Give thanks unto the Lord,</u> for he is good! His faithful love endures forever. Has the Lord redeemed you? *Then speak out! <u>Tell others he has saved you from your enemies.</u>*

Colossians 1:12–14

<u>*Giving thanks*</u> *unto the Father,* who has made us meet [able] to be partakers of the inheritance of the saints in light: Who hath delivered us from the power of darkness, and hath translated us into the kingdom of his dear Son: In whom we have redemption through his blood, even the forgiveness of sins. (KJV)

Confession:

Father God, I give You thanks for making ___(name)___ and me able to partake of our inheritance in Christ Jesus. It is written in Your Word that You have delivered ___(name)___ from the power of darkness (Satan, sickness, and weakness) and brought him/her into Your light (goodness, healing, wholeness, and strength).

CALL OUT TO GOD— HE WILL ANSWER YOU!

Hebrews 4:16

<u>So let us *come boldly to the throne of our gracious God.*</u> There we will *receive* his mercy, and we will find grace to help us when we need it most.

John 15:7 (Jesus speaking)

<u>*"If you abide in Me and My words abide in you, you will ask what you desire,*</u> and it shall be done for you." (NKJV)

Psalms 30:2–5

O Lord my God, *I cried out to you for help,* and you restored *my health.* You brought me up from the grave, O Lord. You kept me from falling into the pit of death. *Sing to the Lord, all you godly ones! Praise his holy name.* For his anger lasts only a moment, but his favor lasts a lifetime! Weeping may last through the night, but joy comes with the morning.

Psalms 30:8–12

I cried out to you, O Lord. *I begged the Lord for mercy,* saying, "What will you gain if I die, if I sink down into the grave? Can my dust praise you from the grave? Can it tell of your faithfulness? *Hear me, Lord, and have mercy on me. Help me, O Lord.*" You have turned my mourning into joyful dancing. You have taken away my clothes of mourning and clothed me with joy, that *I might sing praises to you and not be silent. O Lord my God, I will give you thanks forever!*

James 1:2–8

My friends, be glad, even if you have a lot of trouble. You know that you learn to endure by having your faith tested. But you must learn to endure everything, so that you will be completely mature and not lacking in anything. If any of you need wisdom, you should ask God, and it will be given to you. God is generous and won't correct you for asking. But when you ask for something, you must have faith and not doubt. Anyone who doubts is like an ocean wave tossed around in a storm. If you are that kind of person, you can't make up your mind, and you surely can't be trusted. So don't expect the Lord to give you anything at all. (CEV)

POWER AND PRAYING— USE THE NAME OF JESUS

John 14:12–14 (Jesus speaking)

"I tell you the truth, _anyone who believes in me will do the same works I have done, and even greater works,_ because I am going to be with the Father. _You can ask for anything in my name,_ and I will do it, so that the Son can bring glory to the Father. Yes, _ask me for anything in my name,_ and I will do it!"

John 16:23–24 (Jesus speaking)

"At that time you won't need to ask me for anything. I tell you the truth, _you will ask the Father directly,_ and he will grant your request because you _use my name._ You haven't done this before. _Ask, using my name, and_ you will receive, and you will have abundant joy."

John 15:16 (Jesus speaking)

"<u>You didn't choose me.</u> I chose you. I appointed you to go and produce lasting fruit, so that the Father will give you whatever _you ask for, using my name._"

PEACE

"Fear Not" Is the Most-Often-Given Commandment in the Bible

Isaiah 12:2

See, God has come to save me. <u>_I will trust in him and not be afraid._</u> _The Lord God is my strength and my song;_ he has given me victory. With joy you will drink deeply from the fountain of salvation! In that wonderful day you will sing: "<u>_Thank the Lord! Praise his name! Tell the nations what he has done._</u> <u>Let them know how mighty he is!</u> _Sing to the Lord,_ for he has done wonderful things. _Make known his praise around the world._"

John 14:27

"I am leaving you with a gift—peace of mind and heart. And the peace I give is a gift the world cannot give. *So don't be troubled or afraid.*"

The King James Version says, "'Let not your heart be troubled, neither let it be afraid'" (John 14:27b).

Colossians 3:15a

And *let* the peace that comes from Christ *rule* in your hearts.

Isaiah 26:3

You will guard him and keep him in perfect and constant peace whose mind [both its inclination and its character] is stayed on You, because he commits himself to You, leans on You, and hopes confidently in You. (AMP)

Psalms 4:8

In peace I will lie down and sleep, for you alone, O Lord, will keep me safe.

Confession:

_____(name)_____ and I have the peace of God that passes all understanding keeping our hearts and minds on Jesus. I resist fear in us, and I rebuke it in Jesus' name. We force ourselves to think on good things when bad thoughts try to overtake us.

Psalms 23:4

Even when I walk through the darkest valley, _I will not be afraid,_ for you are close beside me. Your rod and your staff protect and comfort me.

John 14:1 (Jesus speaking)

"_Let not_ your heart be troubled: ye _believe in God, believe also in Me._" (KJV)

2 Timothy 1:7

For God hath not given us the spirit of fear, but of power, and of love, and of a sound mind. (KJV)

Confession:

It is written, God has not given __(name)__ a spirit of fear. We refuse to fear. In Jesus' name, fear must leave me and ___(name)___. God has given us a sound mind and we refuse to fear.

Philippians 4:6–9

Don't worry about anything; instead, *pray about everything. Tell God what you need,* and *thank him for all he has done.* Then you will experience God's peace, which exceeds anything we can understand. His peace will guard your hearts and minds as you live in Christ Jesus. And now dear brothers and sisters, one final thing. *Fix your thoughts on what is true, and honorable, and right, and pure, and lovely, and admirable. Think about things that are excellent and worthy of praise. Keep putting into practice all you learned from me and received from me—everything you heard from me and saw me doing.* Then the God of peace will be with you.

Isaiah 54:14

In righteousness shall you be established, you shall be far from oppression, *for you shall not fear;* and from terror, for it will not come near you. (NIV)

Confession:

Thank You, God, that ___(name)___ is striving to do all You want, so he/she is like the tree planted on the riverbank and will prosper in all he/she does.

Romans 15:13

Now the God of hope fill you with all joy and peace *in believing,* that ye may abound in hope through the power of the Holy Ghost. (KJV)

Confession:

It is written that ___(name)___ be filled with all hope and joy and peace as he/she believes for total healing and we stand on this Word from You, Lord.

THIS IS A SPIRITUAL BATTLE

God wants you well; Satan wants you sick.

God creates everything that is good. The devil creates everything that is evil.

John 10:10–11 (Jesus speaking)

"The thief's [Satan's] purpose is to steal and kill and destroy. My purpose is to give them a rich and satisfying life. I am the good shepherd. The good shepherd sacrifices his life for the sheep."

Confession:

In Jesus' name, the thief cannot steal anything from me or from ___(name)___. All health and wholeness must be restored in the name of Jesus. ___(name)___ will not be killed and will not be destroyed. Thank You, Father, for Your protection and the healing power You have given us through Jesus' dying in our place for our sins. Through Jesus' blood as the living sacrifice for atonement for our sins, ___(name)___ is healed, saved, and delivered from destruction. Praise You, Lord.

2 Corinthians 10:4–5

We use God's mighty weapons, not worldly weapons, to knock down the strongholds of human reasoning and to destroy false arguments. _We destroy every proud obstacle_ that keeps people from knowing God.

James 1:22

But don't just listen to God's word. You must do what it says. Otherwise, you are only fooling yourselves.

1 Peter 2:24

He personally carried our sins in his body on the cross so that we can be dead to sin _and live for what is right._ By his wounds you are healed. Once you were like sheep who wandered away. _But now you have turned to your Shepherd,_ the Guardian of your souls.

(This is a New Testament fulfillment of an Old Testament prophesy.)

3 John 2

Dear Friend, I hope all is well with you and that you are as healthy in body as you are strong in spirit.

Confession:

I believe and confess that ____(name)____'s health is restored even as his/her soul prospers by studying and saying the Word of God.

Exodus 23:25

<u>You must serve only the Lord your God. If you do,</u> I will bless you with food and water, and I will protect you from illness.

Deuteronomy 30:19

Today I have given <u>you a choice</u> between life and death, between blessings and curses. Now I call on heaven and earth to witness <u>the choice you make.</u> Oh, that you would *chose life,* so that you and your descendants might live!

Joshua 1:8–9

This book of the law <u>shall not depart from out of your mouth, but you shall meditate on it day and night, that you may observe to do according to all that is written in it,</u> for then you shall make your way prosperous, and then you shall deal wisely and have good success. Have I not commanded you? _Be strong, vigorous, and very courageous,_ for the Lord your God is with you wherever you go. (AMP)

Romans 12:21

Do not let evil conquer you, but conquer evil by doing good.

Proverbs 3:1–6

My child, _never forget the things I have taught you. Store my commands in your heart._ If you do this, you will live many years and your life will be satisfying. _Never let loyalty and kindness leave you! Tie them around your neck as a reminder. Write them deep within your heart._ Then you will find favor with both God and people, and you will earn a good reputation. _Trust in the Lord with all your heart; do not depend on your own under-standing. Seek His will in all you do,_ and He will show you which path to take.

2 Peter 1:13

So brace up your minds; be sober—morally alert; set your hope wholly and unchangeably on the divine favor that is coming to you when Jesus Christ, the Messiah, is revealed. (AMP)

Isaiah 26:13–14

Oh, Lord, our God, other masters besides you have ruled over us, _but we will acknowledge you and mention your name only._ They [the former tyrant masters are dead, they shall not live and reappear; they are powerless ghosts, they shall not rise and come back.] Therefore, you have visited and made an end of them, and caused every memorial of them [every trace of their supremacy] to perish. (AMP)

Confession:

_God has made this disease/cancer/other as a powerless, dead ghost and has made every remnant of it to disappear. I call things that be not as though they were. This is so in Jesus' name! The healing of ____(name)____ 's body is a documented, medical miracle. Thank You, God! ____(name)____ is cancer free and sickness free, and his/her body is healthy and sound. ____(name)____ has the joy of the Lord as his/her strength, and we sing praises to Your name, Lord._

KIND, FORGIVING, HONEST, GENEROUS PEOPLE ARE BLESSED BY GOD WITH HEALTH

Isaiah 58:7–11

"*Share your food with the hungry, and give shelter to the homeless. Give clothes to those who need them, and do not hide from relatives who need your help.* Then your salvation will come like the dawn, and your wounds will quickly heal. *Your godliness will lead you forward,* and the glory of the Lord will protect you from behind. Then *when you call,* the Lord will answer. 'Yes, I am here,' he will quickly reply. Remove the heavy yoke of oppression. *Stop pointing your finger and spreading vicious rumors! Feed the hungry, and help those in trouble.* Then your light will shine out from the darkness, and the darkness around you will be as bright as noon. The Lord will guide you continually, giving you water when you are dry and restoring your strength. You will be like a well-watered garden, like an ever-flowing spring."

Psalms 1:1–3

Oh, the joys of those *who do not follow the advice of the wicked, or stand around with* sinners, or join in with mockers. But they delight in the law of the Lord, meditating on it day and night. They are like trees planted along the river-bank, *bearing fruit* each season. Their leaves never wither, and they prosper *in all they do.*

Psalms 41:1–3

Oh, the joys of those who are kind to the poor! The Lord rescues them when they are in trouble. The Lord protects them and *keeps them alive.* He gives them prosperity in the land and rescues them from their enemies. *The Lord nurses them when they are sick and restores them to health.*

Proverbs 19:17

If you help the poor, you are lending to the Lord—and he will repay you!

Proverbs 22:9

Blessed are those who are generous, because they feed the poor.

Proverbs 28:27

Whoever gives to the poor will lack nothing, but those who close their eyes to poverty will be cursed.

Confession:

Father, ____(name)____ is a giver to the poor and a tither (10% of gross income to the church), and these Scriptures state that he/she is blessed because he/she has been obedient in these areas. Healing is part of that blessing, and we command that Satan take his hand off that blessing and that it come forth now in Jesus' name.

BUILD YOUR FAITH IN GOD'S FAITHFULNESS RATHER THAN IN YOUR CIRCUMSTANCES AND DOCTORS' REPORTS

Hebrews 11:1–2

Faith is the confidence that what we hope will actually happen; it gives us assurance about the things we cannot see. *Through their faith,* the people in days of old earned a good reputation.

Hebrews 11:6–7

And *it is impossible to please God without faith.* Anyone who wants to come to him *must believe that God exists and that he rewards those who sincerely seek him.* It was by faith that Noah built a large boat to save his family from the flood. He obeyed God, who warned him about things that had never happened before. By his faith Noah condemned the rest of the world, and he received the righteousness that comes by faith.

Romans 10:17

So faith comes from *hearing, that is, hearing the Good News about Christ.*

Mark 11:22–26

Then Jesus said to the disciples, "Have faith in God. I tell you the truth, you can *say to this mountain,* (May you be lifted up and thrown into the sea), and it will happen. *But you must really believe that it will happen and have no doubt in your heart.* I tell you, you can pray for anything, and if you believe that you've received it, it will be yours. But when you are praying, *first forgive anyone* you are holding a grudge against, so that your Father in heaven will forgive your sins, too."

Notice that in Mark 11:23, Jesus said to "<u>say</u> to this mountain" (of cancer or of illness). <u>Words</u> are important in this fight. They are your weapon against the illness in this spiritual battle. Notice, also, that <u>He said not to doubt *in your heart.*</u> There is a difference between doubting in your heart and doubting in your mind. When doubt enters your mind, <u>do not continue to think about it.</u> Force yourself to concentrate on the promises of God, and you will be able to protect your heart from doubting. Satan can only place thoughts in your mind. <u>*It is up to you to resist them and choose not to dwell on negative thoughts.*</u>

1 John 4:4

Ye are of God, little children, and *have overcome* them [evil]: because greater is he that is in you [Jesus/God], than he that is in the world [Satan]. (KJV)

Confession:

It is written, Greater is He that is in
_____(name)_____ *than he that is in the world. Therefore, I command this illness to leave—it*

has no right to be in ___(name)___. Leave, in the strong name of Jesus Christ.

1 Peter 1:5–7

<u>And *through your faith,*</u> God is protecting you by his mighty power until you receive this salvation, which is ready to be revealed on the last day for all to see. <u>*So be truly glad.*</u> There is a wonderful joy ahead, <u>*even though you have to endure many trials for a little while.*</u> <u>These trials will show that your faith is genuine.</u> It is being tested as fire tests and purifies gold—though your faith is far more precious than mere gold. <u>*So when your faith remains strong through many trials,*</u> it will bring you much praise and glory and honor on the day when Jesus Christ is revealed to the whole world.

1 John 5:4

For every child of God defeats this evil world, and *we achieve this victory <u>through our faith.</u>*

Proverbs 3:5–8

<u>*Trust in the Lord with all your heart; do not depend on your own understanding.*</u> <u>*Seek his will in all you do,*</u> and he will show you which path to take. <u>*Don't be impressed with your own wisdom.*</u> Instead, <u>*fear [reverence and worship] the Lord and*</u>

turn away from evil. Then you will have healing for your body and strength for your bones.

Hebrews 4:2

For this good news—that God has prepared this rest—has been announced to us just as it was to them. <u>But it did them no good because they didn't share the faith of those who listened to God.</u>

Hebrews 10:23

<u>Let us hold tightly without wavering to the hope affirm,</u> for God can be trusted to keep his promise.

Hebrews 10:38a

"And *my righteous ones <u>will live by faith.</u>*"

Confession:

Father, ____(name)____ and I hold fast to our confession of faith that You are healing ____(name)____, because we know You are faithful to keep Your Word and promises You gave us in the Bible when we do our part. We confess these Scriptures as You said and remind You of Your promises to ___(name)___ in the Bible. We believe we receive the fulfillment of them in ___(name)___'s life now.

Hebrews 10:35–36

So <u>do not throw away this confident trust in the Lord. Remember the great reward it brings you. Patient endurance is what you need now, so that you will continue to do God's will.</u> Then you will receive all that he has promised.

Jeremiah 32:17

"Oh Sovereign Lord! You have made the heavens and earth by your strong hand and powerful arm. Nothing is too hard for you!"

Consider what Kenneth E. Hagin Sr. says "First, <u>have God's Word</u> for whatever you may be seeking; second, <u>believe God's Word;</u> third, <u>refuse to consider</u> the contradictory circumstances, or what your physical senses may tell you about it; and <u>fourth, give praise to God for the answer.</u> Follow these four steps, and you will always get results. These are four certain steps to deliverance, healing, answered prayer, or whatever you may be seeking from the Lord" ("Faith Versus Feelings", *Kenneth E. Hagin Faith Edition Bible*, [City:Publisher, 1972], emphasis mine).

PASSIONATELY AND PURPOSEFULLY BELIEVE GOD TO HEAL YOU

These Scriptures are our rights through Jesus' death on the cross in our place. However, Satan knows our rights and will steal them if we let him. *You must fight for your rights and those of your loved one.*

Isaiah 53:5

But he was pierced for our rebellion and crushed for our sins. He was beaten so we could be whole. He was whipped so *we could be healed.* All of us, like sheep, have strayed away. <u>We have left God's paths to follow our own.</u> Yet the Lord laid on him the sins *of us all.* (This is an Old Testament prophesy by Isaiah about Jesus Christ.)

Galatians 3:13

But Christ has rescued us from the curse pronounced by the law. When he was hung on the cross, he took upon himself the curse of our wrongdoing. For it is written in the Scriptures, "Cursed is everyone who is hung on a tree." (Note: The curse of the law is every sickness and disease, poverty, and separation from God. See Deuteronomy 28.)

Confession:

Thank You, Lord, for all Your mercy and grace towards me and ____(name)____. Thank You for redeeming ___(name)__ from the hand of the enemy. ___(name)___ is the "redeemed of the Lord" and we say so, as Your Word tells us to do. ____(name)____ is redeemed from sickness, disease, and weakness. ___(name)___ is healthy and whole and strong, in Jesus' name. We are not moved by what we see with our eyes, but by what Your Word says is true. Your Word says that by Jesus' stripes ___(name)__ is healed. Your Word is more real and true than the circumstances we see and hear on this earth. We call things that are not as though they were according to our faith in You—so we call ____(name)____ healed and *whole in Jesus' name. We thank You, Father, for it in Jesus' name.*

Romans 8:11 (speaking to Christians)

The Spirit of God, who raised Jesus from the dead, lives in you. And just as God raised Christ Jesus from the dead, he will give life to your mortal body by this same Spirit living within you.

Confession:

The same Spirit that raised Christ from the dead lives in me and ___(name)___ and gives strength and life to our bodies. Thank You, Holy Spirit, for giving life to ___(name)___'s body now!

Matt 9:28–30

They went right into the house where he [Jesus] was staying, and Jesus asked them, "Do you believe I can make you see?" "Yes, Lord," they told him, "we do." Then he touched their eyes and said, "Because of your faith, it will happen." And their eyes were opened, and they could see!

Mark 5:34b (Jesus speaking)

"Daughter, _your faith_ has made you well. Go in peace. Your suffering is over."

Mark 10:52b (Jesus speaking)

"Go for <u>your faith</u> has healed you."

Luke 17:6b (Jesus speaking)

"<u>If you _had faith_ even as small as a mustard seed, you _could say_ to this mulberry tree (Cancer)</u>, 'May God uproot you and throw you into the sea,' and it would obey you!"

Deuteronomy 7:15

And the Lord will take away from you _all_ sickness. (KJV)

Jeremiah 30:17

"I will give you back your _health and heal your wounds_," says the Lord.

Psalms 118:17

I will not die; instead, I will live to tell what the Lord has done.

Confession:

Thank You, God, that __(name)__ will live and not die and will declare the works of the Lord!

Matthew 8:16–17

That evening many demon-possessed people were brought to Jesus. He cast out the evil spirits *with a simple command, and he healed <u>all</u> the sick.* This fulfilled the word of the Lord through the prophet Isaiah, who said, "He took our sicknesses and removed our diseases."

Confession:

I thank You, Jesus, that I can count on You to always be consistent, and I thank You for performing the same healing miracle for ____(name)____ as You did for people in the Bible. You love us all equally—thank You for loving us!

Some Scriptures refer to illness as an evil spirit that has attacked a person. Pray about casting out that evil spirit that has attacked your loved one. Make sure you study the Bible regarding Matthew

8:16–17, pray, confess your sins, and ask for forgivenss. Then command the evil spirit to leave your loved one in the name of Jesus.

Psalms 126:5–6

Those who <u>plant</u> in tears will harvest with shouts of joy. They weep as they <u>go to plant</u> their seed, but they sing as they return with the harvest.

Confession:

Lord, we may plant our seeds of faith and confession of your Word through tears, but we know we will harvest healing with shouts of joy.

Nahum 1:7–9

The Lord is good, a strong hold in the day of trouble, and he *knoweth those who trust him.* But, with an over-running flood he will make an utter end of the place and darkness shall pursue his enemies. What do you imagine against the Lord? He will make an utter end; *affliction shall not rise up a second time.* (KJV)

SCRIPTURES TO BOOST YOUR HOPE, FAITH, AND STRENGTH

Confession:

Thank You, God, that affliction will NOT rise up a second time. I trust you to heal ____(name)____. You are my stronghold in the day of trouble, and I turn to You for support and help. With Your mighty power You are putting an end to this illness now.

PSALM 91 AS A CONFESSION OF BELIEF AND PRAYER

____(name)____ lives in the shelter of the Most High and finds rest in the shadow of the Almighty. <u>We say of the Lord,</u> He alone is ____(name)____'s refuge, ____(name)____'s place of safety; He is our God, and <u>we are trusting in Him.</u> He will rescue ____(name)____ from every trap and protect ____(name)____ from the fatal plague. He will shield ____(name)____ with His wings. He will shelter ____(name)____ with His feathers. His faithful promises are ____(name)____'s armor and protection. ____(name)____ will not be afraid of the terrors of the night, nor fear the dangers of the day, nor dread the plague that stalks in darkness, nor the disaster that strikes at midday. Though a thousand fall at ___(name)___'s side, though ten thousand are dying around ___(name)___, these evils will not touch ___(name)___. But ___(name)___ will see it with his/her eyes; ___(name)___ will see how the wicked are punished. Because ___(name)___ has made the Lord his/her refuge, and made the Most High his/her shelter, no evil will conquer ___(name)___; no plague will come near his/her dwelling. He orders his angels to protect ___(name)___ wherever he/she goes. They will hold ___(name)___ in their hands to keep ___(name)___ from striking his/her foot on a stone. ___(name)___ will trample down lions and poisonous snakes; ___(name)___ will crush fierce lions and serpents under his/her feet! The Lord says, "I will rescue ___(name)___ because ___(name)___ loves me. I will protect ___(name)___ because he/she trusts in my name. When ___(name)___ calls upon me, I will answer; I will be with ___(name)___ in trouble. I will rescue ___(name)___ and honor ___(name)___. I will satisfy ___(name)___ with a long life and give ___(name)___ my salvation

PASTORAL BLESSING AND FAVOR OF THE LORD

Numbers 6:22–27

May the Lord bless you and protect you. May the Lord smile upon you and be gracious to you. May the Lord show you his favor and give you his peace. (This passage tells what the Lord instructed Aaron [the priest] and his sons to say to bless the people of Israel.)

Job 10:12

"'You gave me life and showed me your unfailing love. My life was preserved by your care.'"

Psalms 5:12

For you bless the godly, O Lord; you surround them with your shield of love.

Confession:

Lord, You have made ____(name)____ right-eous (in right standing) through Jesus Christ; You surround ____(name)____ with the shield of favor and love because he/she walks uprightly in love and forgiveness towards others.

Psalms 41:10

Lord, have mercy on me. Make we well again, so I can pay them back!

Confession:

Because of your favor and mercy on ____(name)____, Lord, You do not let his/her enemies (illness) triumph over him/her.

Confession:

Our trust and hope are in God and God alone; therefore divine favor is ours daily through Jesus Christ.

You have permission to reproduce the Scripture pages for your family members.

EPILOGUE

For further faith building, I listen to Billy Joe Daugherty and Joyce Meyer, as well as other strong Christian leaders, on CDs, and I read their books. Keeping a journal will remind you of what God has already done in your life in the past, which will build your hope and faith in future miracles and answered prayers.

"Those who live only to satisfy their own sinful nature will harvest decay and death from that sinful nature. But those *who live to please the Spirit will harvest everlasting life* from the Spirit. *So let's not get tired of doing what is good. At just the right time, we will reap a harvest of blessing if we don't give up.* Therefore, whenever we have the opportunity, we should *do good to everyone*—especially to those in the family of faith" (Galatians 6:8–10 NLT).

Continually fight this battle spiritually to win this war!

Health and faith be yours, through the strong name of our Lord, Jesus Christ. God bless you!

APPENDIX

JUDY BUTLER'S PRIORITY PRAYER SHEET

1. The healing power of God is working mightily in Judy's body effecting a healing and a cure: driving out cancer, diverticulitis, and all manner of sickness and disease.

2. The anointing destroys the yoke of cancer in Judy's body (Isaiah 10:27).

3. Judy has healing and health, prosperity and wealth, wisdom, knowledge, and understanding.

4. Judy has the peace of God that passes all understanding (Philippians 4:7).

5.   Judy has the joy of the Lord as her strength (Nehemiah 8:10).

6.   Judy is cancer free. Judy is diverticulitis-free. Her colon is healthy and sound.

7.   Judy will live and not die and will declare the works of the Lord (Psalms 118:17).

8.   This healing of Judy's body is a documented, medical miracle. We call those things that be not as though they were (Romans 4:17).

Short-term prayer needs: infection to leave, temperature to be normal, no post-surgery pain or problems.

HOSPITAL ROOM SUPPLY CHECKLIST

✓ Continuous-play cassette or CD player.

✓ Cassettes or CDs of scriptural songs (David Ingles, Sharon Daugherty).

✓ Cassettes or CDs of healing Scriptures (John Hagee or Kenneth Hagin Sr. are good choices).

✓ Notebook for tracking dates and times of medications, breathing practices, and exercises completed. Also monitor dates and times of problems that arise, personality changes, mood changes, and pain or spasms, which can then be compared to changes in medications. Track what is eaten, when, and the amounts eaten.

✓ Pens, magic markers, highlighters, and stationery.

✓ Notebook for phone messages and visitor/flower logs.

✓ Comfortable pajamas.

✓ Snacks your fighter usually likes.

✓ Applesauce, bananas, tea, peanut butter (protein), and protein bars.

✓ Blankets.

✓ Clean socks and underwear.

✓ Robe or coat for going to see the doctor or to take treatments.

✓ This book and others on healing (Billy Joe Daugherty, Kenneth Hagin Sr., Dodie Osteen, Charles Capps, and Joyce Meyer are good positive authors with materials on healing).

✓ Bible (a version that is easy to understand like the New Living Translation).

✓ Priority Prayer Sheet (keep it updated and distribute to your church and prayer partners).

✓ List of friends/family phone numbers and long-distance calling cards.

✓ List of friends who will stay with your loved one in your place and whom your loved one would feel comfortable staying with overnight.

✓ Pretty "victory" flowers.

✓ Large photos of your loved one when he or she was healthy so he or she can focus on what he or she is aiming for.

✓ Friendly "No Visitors" signs that you can make as needed.

✓ Dirty clothes bag and suitcase.

✓ Personal toiletries for your loved one—especially lotion.

YOUR PERSONAL NOTES

HEALING TO-DO CHECKLIST FOR YOUR LOVED ONE

✓ Play positive ministry, worship, or Scripture cassettes or CDs continuously unless the medical staff is there or you are confessing Scriptures.

✓ Do not waste time watching non-encouraging TV or videos.

✓ Track everything—this will help you and the medical staff notice allergies to medications, problems in the treatment plan, and things that work well.

✓ Massage lotion into your fighter's feet and hands to soothe them.

✓ A personal touch is comforting.

✓ Keep noise level as low as possible, as noise causes stress.

✓ Minimize the number of visitors to only two to three at a time, and do not let visitors in who will be loud or stressful for your loved one to see. Germs from others can be dangerous for your loved one.

✓ Limit visitors and ask them to leave when you see your loved one is tired or starting to become stressed. *You* are the protector of your loved one, and he or she is depending on you!

✓ Ring the nurse when a monitor starts beeping; notice when an IV bag becomes low and alert the staff.

✓ Be cognizant of food intake and ask for nutritional supplements (health shakes, IV nutrients) if your loved one's weight is low.

✓ Know staff members by name and treat them with respect, but ask for what you need and know what is being done.

✓ If possible, have someone your loved one is comfortable with be with him or her at all times, because even the best hospital staffs make mistakes—they are human, too. Train those covering for you in what to look for and what to do.

✓ When pain occurs, ask for more pain medication. Know at what intervals it can be given, and watch the clock. You have only one patient to keep up with, but the nurse may have fifteen. You can ensure better care and less pain for your loved one if you do this. If one pain medication isn't working, ask the nurse to page the doctor for another kind. If your loved one is vomiting up the pills, ask for a shot or IV painkiller instead. Your loved one needs the pain medicine to get into his or her system.

✓ Be sure your fighter is getting plenty of protein, which builds the immune system. If your fighter won't eat what is presented by the hospital, ask the nurse for other food options.

✓ Try to smile and laugh together about happy memories. Laughter is good medicine for the soul.

✓ Say all the nice things you always intended to tell your loved one.

✓ Confess the Scriptures and Scriptural confessions over your fighter, or have your fighter read these words aloud continually throughout each day. *This* is God's medicine for your fighter. Have him or her nod or say, "I agree," after each one, if possible. Tell God how much you love Him, and pray and praise Him together in the hospital room many times throughout the day.

✓ Tell your fighter encouraging words and that you love him or her.

✓ Hold your loved one's hand. Kiss your loved one's cheek. Cry with him or her.

✓ Do not remind your loved one of pain, fear, or other negative things he or she has gone through—and don't let others do so. *This is not helpful* and only causes more pain and fear.

✓ Let your fighter talk and verbally process thoughts and feelings, and keep his or her words in secret. Be your loved one's confidant.

✓ Smile when you are with your loved one. You are the only source of joy in your loved one's life so determine to give him or her joy and peace.

✓ Know how to dress a bandage, work the pain pump, etc.

✓ Be sure you and your fighter are confident in the doctors. If not, change doctors at once.

✓ Encourage your fighter to sleep when possible, and keep the cassettes or CDs of healing Scriptures and songs playing softly, yet loudly enough for your fighter to understand the words.

✓ Request to be moved to a room with a window—sunlight adds peace and comfort. Rooms without windows cause mental confusion over time.

✓ Hospital walls are dismal. Bring in a favorite painting, family photos, and flowers.

✓ Bring in foods your loved one likes or have your relief person bring some on the way to relieve you, or cook your loved one's favorite recipe.

✓ Make sure you get rest and sleep. Request sleeping pills if needed from your doctor. If you lose your strength, you will not be much help for your loved one. If you get sick, you should not see your loved one, because his or her immune system may be very weak.

✓ No sick visitors or relief persons allowed— no exceptions.

✓ Talk about your fighter's favorite things— vacations, places, foods, friends, memories, photos, events, sports—for relaxation or to take your fighter's mind off of the pills he or she just swallowed.

✓ Talk about what your fighter wants to do and where your fighter wants to go when he or she is healed. This gives your fighter something fun to look forward to and gives him or her refreshed hope. Plan to "Go and do" like Jesus suggests in Mark 10:52b and in Mark 5:34b. Plan to LIVE and GO and DO!

✓ Sing your loved one's favorite positive songs, if he or she would like that.

✓ Keep frozen dinners and paper plates at home for you to eat on the run without much fuss. The easier and faster, the better.

✓ Ask for a cot for you or your relief to sleep on in your fighter's room each night. You may want to bring your own pillow.

✓ Sweatpants and shirts are easy "pajamas" for you.

YOUR CHECKLIST ADDITIONS

_____

_____

_____

_____

_____

_____

_____

_____

_____

_____

_____

_____

_____

_____

_____

_____

_____

_____

MEDICATIONS, FOOD, WATER, SUPPLEMENTS, IVS, ETC SCHEDULE

Date	Time Given	Dosage

Name of Med, Food, Supplement, IV, Water

TIME DUE AGAIN

YOUR PRAYER REQUESTS

Your Prayer   Victory & date

Your Prayer	Victory & date

ABOUT THE AUTHOR AND
BUTLER MINISTRY FOUNDATION

If you would like notices of future materials as they become available, please contact us at BMF, PO Box 700686, Tulsa, OK 74170.

We donate these and other materials to organizations for people in need. If you would like to contribute, please mail your tax-deductible donations made payable to BMF to us at the above address. Be sure to include your return mailing address for your receipt to be mailed to you.

To purchase copies of this book, please go to www.caregiverstrength.com, www.Amazon.com, Barnes and Noble, or special order them from your local bookstore.

Made in the USA
Coppell, TX
21 December 2024

43293116R00066